unexpected turn

unexpected turn

Jim Sagel

UNIVERSITY OF NEW MEXICO PRESS
ALBUQUERQUE

Library of Congress
Cataloging-in-Publication Data

Sagel, Jim
Unexpected turn/Jim Sagel. — first edition
p.   cm.
ISBN 0-8263-1823-1 (pbk.)
I. Title
PS3569.A32U54 1997   97-4632
818'.5408 — dc21
CIP

*Some of these writings originally appeared in
differing forms in the following publications:*

Blue Mesa Review
No. Four, Spring 1992

El Palacio
Summer 1993

Foreplay and French Fries
Mango Publications, 1981

GuestLife New Mexico, 1994–95

Río Grande Review
Fall 1992

Sell-Outs
Winter 1992

Tamaqua
*Fall 1992, Winter 1992
and Spring 1993*

The Guadalupe Review
No. One, 1991

CONTENTS

unexpected turn

Pass with Care, the sign cautions, but you need no reminding as you pass a butte brooding over stego-saurus hills. You know that the next turn promises the unexpected—a Ponderosa laid open by light-ning, a herd of cattle sleek as a Brahman vision, a lake tremulous with trout. This is a land where the sky intoxicates the eye, and history gossips in the willows lining the great river. It's the lost roads that lead to desert gardens; you miss your turn and end up finding your way.

You turn your eyes to the ridge above the pueblo and gaze at the deer dancers descending in the icy dawn. You turn on the dance floor in your lover's arms, as the *músicos* play the *valses* their grand-fathers learned from their grandfathers. You turn a hoe over in the mud to make the adobes for the home you are already plastering in your dreams. You turn your head just long enough for the *abuelo*, the grotesque and guffawing trickster, to steal your hat, leaving you to squint at the *Matachines* dancing their masked ritual. You turn over in your hands the *santo* that has emerged from the root of a cotton-

wood tree; you trace the water serpent coiled around
a pot burnished black as an unbroken memory.

Once you have known this land, you will always
turn back. Like the exiled poet who could sense
his lover combing her hair from a thousand miles
away, you will always hear the drum pounding in
your pulse, the *Llorona* weeping in your inner ear,
the cranes flapping their wings alongside the river in
your blood. Once you have taken the unexpected
turn, you will never again pass without caring.

blind curve

WHEN THE *ZACATE*
GREW WILD IN THE *LLANOS*

Leaving the fiesta, I walk through a field of freshly
cut alfalfa. *Yo vendo unos ojos negros,* the singer's
voice reverberates in a distant box: "Black eyes for
sale," but I'm not buying. All I want to do is smell
the brittle fragrance of the cut hay, the end of the
summer smell of the last cut that takes me twenty
Augusts back to a time when the timothy hay
undulated like a yellow tidal wave in the wind and
we stacked a thousand bales under the sweltering
sun, you and I—powerful *viejo* and college refugee.

That evening, as you sharpened your pocketknife
in the glow of a kerosene lamp and told tales in the
tongue of your *abuelos* of the days when the *zacate*
grew wild in the *llanos,* I collapsed into a primitive
sleep on a dusty *colchón.* When I awoke the follow-
ing morning, you were already boiling fresh coffee
in the water you had carried up from the stream.

As you fried eggs and potatoes over the wood fire,
I felt an appetite grow so big inside me, I needed
two languages to express it. *Al fin sabía lo que era el
hambre.* At last I had found what I was hungering for.

ESTRELLA FUGAZ

I am thinking of the space between the stars when
a tail of fire abruptly blazes in the San Ildefonso sky.
Just so unpredictably did I tumble from orbit, my
identity engulfed in flames. Yet, my only wish is to
fall out of myself again and again.

The new H.U.D. houses in Santa Clara Pueblo are
laid out in a line straight as a parochial school ruler.
But, then, there are no better Catholics in the New
World than the Tewa Indians. Probably no better
Baptists either. Still, it is not the Pope but Po'pay
whose spirit beats in the kiva. Though succeeding
generations of Tewas may live at right angles in
English, their children's children will continue
to dance the Corn Dance in front of the church.
And even if the world comes to an end, the Pueblo
Governor will refuse to grant an easement for
the Second Coming of Christ.

VOLVER

Y *volver, volver, voool-ver,* we wail at the sweat-
drenched moon in a Santa Fe parking lot, arms
linked around waists in an inebriated chain swaying
against gravity with Flaco Jiménez whose accordion
bursts open in a flood of electrified joy that sweeps
us back and back to that first kiss under a sky equally
drunken with stars, *y volver a tus brazos otra vez,*
back to the first time, fingers trembling, heart
howling just behind the lips.

ANCESTRAL STEW

Certain Amazonian hunters commemorate
their dead by cremating them and ritualistically
consuming their pulverized bones in a banana stew.
The thought of an ancestor decaying beneath the
earth is abhorrent to these Indians who believe the
soul cannot be at peace until the body has found a
final resting place in the cells of those it once
engendered.

In just such a way your words have taken up
residence in my DNA, your stories spiraling
through the double helix of my soul. Bare-
boned as my retelling of your tales may be,
I offer them to all who would eat.

JESUS IN THE TORTILLA

The Turn-off Ahead leads to Lake Arthur, a white
clapboard mirage on the fringes of *la Jornada del
Muerto* where Spanish colonists left their bones in
the seventeenth century, and Los Alamos scientists
set the sands ablaze at a site they dubbed "Trinity."
Not far from the spot where the tower that cradled
the "gadget" evaporated, a Lake Arthur woman
turned a tortilla over on her blackened *comal* one
Cold War morning and discovered the face of Christ
burned into the surface of the unleavened bread.
Visitors are allowed only twice a year on strictly
supervised tours of Ground Zero, but you can
stop any time to gawk at the holy dough
preserved under glass like the Grail.

RUNOFF

Braced against the current, I battle the swollen creek
for a foothold on these rocks polished by the water's
desire for the sea, the same insatiable thirst that
surges through my blood.

CONJUGATION

Llueve. It is raining in Spanish, each drop a pure "o"
splattering into diminutive vowels—*gotitas* that roll
melodically off the roof of the abandoned adobe.
There are no consonants in the autumn rain dis-
solving these walls built by a husband and wife
married now in the dust.

Still, the polysyllabic *lluvia* repeats their story.
La tierra—it splashes like a lover wetly murmuring
in your ear. *La tierra*—the sky still falling for the
earth in a timeless conjugation of corrosion and
rebirth.

Death is a noun, the rain murmurs, but to love is
forever a verb.

BLIND CURVE

Leading the caravan, a pickup labors under a
mountainous load of firewood, its tires wavering in
past tense. All I can do is slow down and notice the
stream that straddles the road is running off with the
sunrise—understand that for the "ultimate in no-
frills dining," I will have to pull off at the Lovato
Burger Drive-in. But I don't stop, even though the
next sign says, "Jesus is coming," and three teen
angels swing their voluptuous legs in unison from
the tailgate of a Toyota 4 x 4 in the shade of a
mammoth cottonwood. I follow the lurching truck
past escarpments of granite still glowing from the
Big Bang; past the *descanso* with its five white
crosses and plastic roses marking the spot where
Juan—simply "Juan"—left his surname in the
wreckage of his body; past Ducky's Meats special-
izing in hay, custom slaughtering and choke cherry
jelly; past a bent-backed couple walking hand in
gnarled hand with poles baited for rainbows.
Rounding a blind curve, I realize the truck full
of firewood has vanished with my loneliness.

SAINT-MAKER

Alone in his workshop in the sierra, the *santero*
broods over his chisels and rasps, searching for the
face of God in a fallen tree while a holy extravagance
of light pours through the window.

BARBECHANDO

Ay, Diosito, si borracho te ofendí,
En la cruda me sales debiendo.
Gustavo A. Santiago, *"La Cruda"*

Early on the morning of the worst hangover in my
life, you had me plowing behind the skittery old
mare. Head pounding and internal organs churning,
I wrestled that iron tooth as it gnawed into the
ground. What original sin had I committed,
I wondered, unable to remove my aching hands from
the plow to wipe away the rivers of sweat burning in
my eyes. Yet, as I hauled on the reins at the end of
the row to turn the mare back into the sun, I saw the
potatoes, white jewels lying in the broken earth.
And all of the family hunched over in the field like
drunken pirates filling gunny sacks with treasure.

MAJOR SLIDE

Like that cloud snagged on the pleistocene teeth of
the ridge, you are lodged in my cerebrum. To forget
you now would require a second ice age, a geologic
upheaval in my corpuscles. There's a major slide
ahead, a roadblock at every synapse. Rolling down
my window, I am not surprised to find you directing
traffic.

BUSCANDO MELODÍA

Estoy buscando melodía para tener cómo llamarte.
Silvio Rodríguez

It's impossible as the New Mexican sky, this need to
name your beauty. Language, like the eye, is limited
by the horizon: even poetry falls short of this edge.

So, like the Cuban poet, I am searching for a
melody. It must be a melody of apples and moon-
light, a melody inevitable as your eyes. A cirrus
fugue in the Cerrillos sky. The Gregorian chant of
the stars beyond the stars above Picurís. Sandhill
cranes tracking sad lyrics in the marshes of the
Bosque del Apache. Lightning ripping a blues riff
out of the heart of the Acoma night. The sonata
of the cicadas at dawn in San Cristóbal. Half moon
melting in a nocturne of liquid notes on Heron
Lake.

I am casting under sun-tinged clouds for the melody
that will tremble free of this page like my fingers
when I trace the memory of your smile.

PEANUTS ARE FOR SALE

Peanuts are for sale at the Sun Dale Ranch on
the road to the Melrose Bombing Range, the same
highway that leads half a century later to the ruins of
Hiroshima that still smolder just beyond those grain
elevators mushrooming in the livid sky.

UNTOUCHABLE

All you want me to bring back is a rock. No gifts,
no fine words—not even these. But you must
understand I have spent a lifetime making my way
to the edge of this stream where I sit in the spent
leaves writing what I know cannot be written. As
twilight thickens over my fingers, I realize these
words are falling short of the page. At last I see
your stone, luminescent in the gurgling darkness.
Forgive me for returning empty-handed, but if
I touch it now, I may never get home.

ONE PERCENT SOLUTION
—for Michael

On the lake where the eagle makes his nest, you tell
me you shouldn't be alive. One hundred times that
grenade tumbles out of the night and rolls into your
hand. Ninety-nine times you'd be a dead man, you
say. Who shakes hands with Death and survives?

On the way here we passed the Vietnam Memorial,
but you didn't want to stop. "There's nothing there
for me to see," you said without irony, hungry to get
on the lake where you once netted spawning shad by
the dozens with your father—poles cast aside in the
canoe, the two of you scooping silver currency from
the waters.

As we float into the canyon, you remember how you
watched twenty-five inch lunkers striking your bait,
long before your father wandered away in the flooded
gorges of his memory and the night made off with
your eyes. But you shook on it, your fingers fused in
those shrapnel knuckles. You wouldn't renege now,
even if you could pull your hand back—even if you
knew the knot that would tie your optic nerve

together again. How could you trade the family you have never seen for the sight of no wife, no daughters?

Smiling in the sunrise, you cast your line that floats high over the dark jungle on this dazzling one in a hundred morning.

WARNING FOR WEAVING

*The last few miles you veered into the oncoming lane
at least three times*—the state patrolman says. Good
thing he hasn't been following me the last few years.
I have always driven to extremes—taking on the
patch of black ice, ignoring every *Do Not Enter*,
racing head-long into the most treacherous curves
in the road. Just a warning for weaving this time,
but as soon as I have left the law behind, I go right
back to my swerving. I have never had much use
for the center line.

CHACO

Standing within walls that have stood since
the Dark Ages, I kneel to lace my tennis shoes
and discover a pottery shard overlooked by
the thousands of tourists who race for cover
the moment it begins to rain. Only when the
drops strike the shard in my palm do I under-
stand the sky means to wash me away.

CALAVERAS

High on this ridge in the Jémez Mountains,
the story has it, two bull elk locked horns and
died in an instinctual embrace, their skulls two
bleached moons intertwined on the forest floor.
What snarl of language can name the dark beauty
of our own collision?

COYOTE AND THE CAMPER

The dead dog spawning flies in front of the Sacred
Heart Church is no more incongruous than the
satellite dish sandwiched between a crumbling pair
of adobe houses up the road nor the salty-bearded
logger sitting in the nearby *cantina*, sharing a Miller
Lite with his neighbor who's been secretly screwing
his wife. Coyote, the Indians say, had a hand in
shaping this land, but he never would have been
foolish enough to get caught beneath the wheels
of a camper.

A soft rain awaited us along with the *músicos* as
we entered our courtyard, newly remarried but with
the old elopement in our eyes. Surrounded by the
family we once left behind, we danced *el valse de los
novios* on the darkening flagstone. Twirling under an
umbrella, I held you with the tenderness of our first
morning alone, and the violin waltzed into the
clouds.

Weary of words, I loosen the last bolt on the pressure
plate in the cinderblock shop, remembering in Span-
ish the smell of sawdust and crankshaft oil, the *cuentos*
you told as we replaced the transmission in the old
Ford tractor, the *versos* you sang as we rebuilt the
engine in my long-suffering truck, my overalls caked
with grease, content as I may never be again. The
music of your language is still with me as I work
wordlessly with your *llaves gastadas*, these wrenches
worn smooth by your hands. It was the horse stories
you loved best, even as we grappled so stubbornly
with internal combustion, even as you lay the last
time in that hospital bed. *"Quítame este barandal,"*
you said, straining at the steel rails like a stallion
against a fence—"Take off these racks, I'm ready to
go." But I'm still here in your silent shop, struggling
to replace the clutch in this foreign car.

JACKPILE

Half moon hanging over Paguate, a disembodied
landscape of ashen mounds, earth unearthed like
a secret finally found out a decade after the last
yellow cakes of death were stripped from this soil
where the granddaughter of a Laguna miner who
died of cancer swings in a vacant playground,
rising higher and higher until the toes of her
tennis shoes graze the ragged edge of the moon.

Approaching Milagro on a Sunday afternoon,
my eye is struck by the image of three antiquated
telephone poles looming over a gravelly swell.
Flooring the accelerator, I pass the latter-day
Golgotha and the ocean liner of a car I have
been following for miles. "Jesus" reads a fish
embossed on the rear panel above the model
name, "Grand Marquis."

Inside the "clean restrooms" faithfully advertised
by the Milagro Chevron, three different types of
condoms are available from a gleaming white
dispenser. *Evening Magic* and *Treasure Chest* are
seventy-five cents a piece, but, for only a quarter
more, you can take home a *Nite Glow*: "Turn out
the lights and watch the glow grow and grow."

Continuing west at speeds well beyond the limit,
I scatter a trio of ravens who rise from a roadkill
on incorruptible wings.

AFTERBIRTH

"You can only live so long."
The last line sung by Richard Versalle, a tenor who
suffered a fatal heart attack on the stage
of the Metropolitan Opera House

The mud plaster was still wet on the walls in
the house you were building when your heart shut
down. Mute, we stood with folded arms around the
altar she constructed for you using feathers, photo-
graphs, fishing lures, and earth from the place where
you fell. Afterwards, we emerged from that adobe
womb, startled by the light, the smell of clay
clinging like afterbirth to our clothes.

SACRAMENTO

The sun sets over the Sacramentos, igniting a cholla cactus outside my window. If only it would speak, even in riddles, like the first burning bush. There is no silence denser than that of a motel room in the desert at dusk.

Root beer floats *abuelo* bought at the A&W on the
way to the drive-in, drink them fast before all the ice
cream melts while Godzilla tramples Japanese cities
under a sky foaming with moonlit clouds.

Tucked into the window space above the rear seat
of the car, I sleep all the way home with celluloid
buffalo stampeding through my head, but watch out
if Dad steps on the brakes too hard because down
you'll go, rolling right out of your dreams.

Four of us huddled in the trunk of the car, we sneak
past the gate and emerge like Trojan Horse soldiers
once we are inside, taking no prisoners as we attack
the case of cheap *cerveza*.

Alice's Restaurant is playing, but I'm too busy try-
ing to navigate the stick shift of the VW bug while
unbuttoning her blouse to pay much attention, and,
anyway, I've already seen it before, though I was too
stoned to remember what happened.

Laughing like *locos* at Cantinflas on double-feature night, we munch handfuls of piñón and turn the speaker all the way up so Papá who is deaf, at least when he doesn't want to hear, can hear.

The Yucca has closed its gates for good in Santa Fe; likewise, the Kit Carson Drive-in Theatre in Taos. And now the Starlighter no longer exists. To add the worst kind of insult to the injury, they've started to slice up the land for homesites, some of which may be sold to couples conceived in this very place under the thirty-five millimeter gaze of María Félix and Humphrey Bogart. The Starlighter Subdivision: one more sign of our joyless times.

FISHING WITH CHUANG TZU

Crouched in broom-tail grasses, I cast a fly over
waters only recently freed from mountain ice.
On a day two thousand years ago blazing with
sunlight like this one, Chuang Tzu went walking
alongside the Hao River with his friend and
metaphysical angler, Hui Tzu.

*How the fish are enjoying themselves as they go
flashing through the water!* observed Chuang Tzu.

But you are no fish, said Hui Tzu, always the
empiricist. *How can you know the fish are happy?*

*And you are no Chuang Tzu. How can you know that
I do not know the happiness of the fish?* Chuang Tzu
replied as my pole starts dancing under the trout-
back sky.

THE SYNTAX OF SEPARATION

He speaks in vague pronouns, deliberately muddy-
ing the antecedents. She replies in fragments.
Shifting tense. With her eyes. From the lips of the
Cerro Pedernal like a misplaced modifier the setting
sun dangles. Anything to avoid saying goodby.

where the road deadends

*El punto final es pequeñito, y casi no se le ve
en la página escrita; se le advierte luego por contraste,
cuando después de él comienza el blanco.*
Julio Cortázar, *Diario de Andrés Fava*

The road deadends at our Lady of Sorrows Church
where a blue-robed Virgin beckons me to surrender
to the amnesia inside. Shifting at the last moment,
I turn toward the hills and search for your smile in
the rocks.

Climbing the face of a mesa, I remember it is I who is tumbling through space and not the sun. I write these lines wrestling the wind over a sheet of paper as my car dwindles in the distance, the final period before the whiteness begins.

Once I scaled a mountain with rope, hammer and
pitons. You were in the lead. I was below, in love
with your wife and you knew it. You insisted on the
climb—she cajoled me into believing that risking
my life on the rocks would "clear the air."

I began climbing in the abstract, struggling up the
granite wall behind you for something I would have
called love in those heady times. But as I battled for
breath, I realized it was my blood streaming from
my broken knuckles, my body I saw blooming like
a dark flower on the rocks two hundred feet below
if I missed a single foothold.

You had warned me to pull down, not out, as I
jammed my fingers into the fissures in the rocks,
but panic, by then, had overcome me. When that
boulder groaned towards me, I screamed, "Tension!"
desperately embracing the mountain that meant
to repel me. You plucked me past the danger, of
course, pulling on the rope that was my umbilical
cord. I still cannot remember reaching the summit.

Several years later, over numerous beers and a
rambling discussion of your divorce, you told me
you had nearly let me fall that day. In an instant,
you had balanced rage against guilt in a calculation
no mortal should have to make. You clasped your
heavy arm around my neck then at the bar—
everything had worked out well, she was no good
for either one of us, still, you could just as easily
have let me fall off the mountain, you just wanted
to let me know.

Every few feet I pause to pick up another sunburned stone while a raven appraises my ceremony from a lapis sky. *Your carnelian hair danced in the yellow wind*, I write, scrambling higher as the rocks pile up on the page. How will I ever reach the top lugging along all these colors?

Pulling myself over the final ridge, I discover the
shrine that called me from the church below. Yet,
even within this circular wall of stones there is no
escaping the wind. I have reached the summit but
your breath still rages in my ears.

right of way

FISSURE

Los Alamos physicists show off pottery shards
collected in their back yards, the fractured remains
of vessels once used by the ancestors of Pueblo
Indians who now commute up the hill to guard,
cook and clean for those same cloistered technocrats
whose coming signaled not only the end of the war
but the close of an era of self-sufficiency in the
pueblos and Hispanic villages of northern New
Mexico whose fertile croplands have been split into
subdivided lots where old men sit in their back yards
and dream of lost harvests in the language now
foreign to their grandchildren.

DEMOLITION

Two men in Stetsons and stainless overalls tear apart
a barn for the beams which will eventually perch on
Santa Fe adobe walls as uncomfortably as a Lubbock
fisherman sitting on the end stool at the El Norteño
Bar and Club. They strain with crowbars and rip at
the weathered lumber with power saws as if the soul
could be transferred like a skin graft, as though the
old pine heart of the vigas won't continue to grieve
for the sky.

WHITE SANDS

I trace a circle in this desiccated sea, but a grain
of sand has lodged, like your absence, in my eye.
My vision blurs as half of my world evaporates in the
white wind. Without you, I am a sad hemisphere,
a sand dune drifting south of the stars.

CROSSOVER

Pues, si es usté la muerte, está muy flaca.
—from *"La comadre Sebastiana," Cuentos españoles
de Colorado y Nuevo México*, Juan B. Rael

I ran into him in the plumbing section at the local
hardware store. The stories had been circulating for
some time, yet I wasn't prepared for the fleshless-
ness of his face. He had at last crossed over, but this
woman had a skeletal handshake. We skirted it with
remarkable skill, talking about the weather and the
whereabouts of mutual friends. At the register we
laughed at the coincidence: both of us, it turned
out, were buying replacement traps.

Coming off the mountain with a load of two
hundred aspen *latillas*, I shifted down past the
canyon where a witch once collided with our
windshield in the form of a fireball, past the mud-
chinked log cabin where we spent a few precious
nights in the previous century, past that opening
in the forest where we cut the thick cedars I would
split for our ceiling.

Removing my sweat-stained hat in exhaustion,
I felt a surge of the joy that sometimes set you
singing the old songs of your youth. Though the
moment twirled away like a dance partner on a
sawdusted floor, I drove on in a state of wonder,
amazed at the fact that I was there, right there in
that truck backfiring past the oaks and the pines,
and, in that rare instant, I understood I was already
older than the rest of my life.

BREAKING SUN

The breaking sun strikes the pottery shards pressed
into the plaster at the base of the window, an open
wound in the east wall of our house, the clay vessel
that, like the shattered confines of the flesh, fails to
contain the light that keeps rushing back to the light.

HAPPY BEYOND REASON

Happy beyond reason, I walk through the rain
washing the sun out of the Talpa sky. Knowing
I would be the first to fly off the planet this evening,
I offer silent thanks to the force of gravity as I
wander over glistening mats of pine needles and
berries. Settling on the stump of an aspen, I laugh
aloud at the water pouring off the brim of my hat.
Without warning, my saturated heart bursts free of
my chest, startling several meadowlarks as it goes
careening through the pines.

RIGHT OF WAY

—en memoria de don Jesús

A muffler lies naked, bleeding rust in the center of
Canyon Road, forcing Range Rovers and BMW's to
swerve around it. Less than a block away, Jesús Ríos
loads a truck with piñón, surrounded by the seven-
figured adobe homes and art galleries that have
mushroomed around him over the last half century.
Just this morning, don Jesús refused the latest offer
to sell out the Ríos Wood and Freight Service with
his perennial—only the amount escalates over the
years—response: "They wanted to give me three
million dollars but I told them: *That's not enough
for this Mexican.*"

Perhaps the land developer didn't notice don Jesús
only removed one of his pitch-stiffened work gloves
in order to shake hands, and chances are one of the
patriarch's many sons or grandsons or even a great-
grandson will pick the muffler up, but that doesn't
mean they will ever get out of the way.

ON NIGHTS LIKE THESE
ONCE LIT BY THE MOON

The old apple orchards are ripening with double-
wides, their windows digitally lit by the Shopping
Channel. How quickly I have come to live too long,
I think, as I drive through the night like a man
turning the pages of a family album filling up
with pictures of the dead.

THE KING

Visit the King, reads the sign at La Iguana Art
Gallery, located on the narrow banks of the Río
Grande above Velarde. The gallery owner herself,
it seems, received a royal visitation when the spirit
of Elvis, embodied in a silver *milagro,* caused her
colon cancer to go into remission.

And why shouldn't Elvis make a housecall in these
wildly isolated villages where the *Santo Niño* wears
out pair after pair of shoes on his nocturnal rounds
watching over the children of Chimayó? In the early
years of the century, Christ himself walked through
these mountains named after his blood, healing
scores of the sick, including our elderly landlord
who claimed *el Sanador* had raised him from his
deathbed as a child, though his narration of the
tale was continuously interrupted by coughing
due to his terminal emphysema.

La Iguana is now "For Sale by Owner," I notice
as I drive up the canyon where the river still runs
with its original passion. One can only hope the
King has not decided to be cruel in the heart of
these mountains where faith remains so true.

STONE VIRGIN

Like the Virgin painted on a boulder in Arroyo de
Agua, you hover overhead on granite wings. It is
your beauty that holds you so reverentially aloft.
Lady in endless waiting, you are surrounded by an
otherworldly glow. If only your worshipers knew
how desperately your body burns for him.

THE NINTH MINT

Last night over blackened catfish and Tecates,
I was witness to a seventeenth wedding anniversary
celebration in the booth beside me at a seafood
restaurant on the Mexican border. Rotund and
radiant, she fondled the seventeen long-stemmed
red roses lying on the table next to a plate heaped
with lobster carcasses and shrimp tails. Reflexively
flexing the crab-crackers in his hand, he thanked
her, honey, for the cassette tape of "easy-listening
classics" and the seventeen, you're so sweet,
darling, after-dinner mints.

Today, as my car is so badly pummeled by the
mesquite-whipping wind that I nearly flatten a
patriotic hitchhiker waving a miniature American
flag instead of his thumb, I remember that obese
couple and the two Indian women—a mother and
daughter, I imagined—who, with scores of the poor,
filtered through the three lanes of traffic backed
up on the international bridge between Ciudad

Juárez and El Paso. Dressed in their *rebozos* and embroidered *huipiles*, they were hawking, in one hand, a crucified Christ. In the other, they offered a Batman Halloween costume.

Though I have left the border behind, I can't help wondering which of those two gods was the first to sell. And who got to eat that ninth mint when they divided them up after dinner?

SKIPPING STONES

Leaning against a moss-laden fir, I skip rocks across a stream with you in my mind, *piedras como monedas,* spare change of the heart, jumping once, twice, three times over the surface of my memory that, like this water, is devastatingly clear. The secret is in the release. Let go at just the right moment, and the stone will skip free of the water and fly.

Each night is a little death, as we abandon ourselves to dreams on this cast-iron bed your parents gave us at the beginning of our lives together, the same bed they had received nearly half a century before as their own wedding gift.

When it came into our lives, the black posters were missing one of their brass balls which your father replaced with a hand-carved wooden one fashioned with selfless beauty, like a love poem written for the one who will never see it.

This bed in which you were conceived is the place I would choose to die my true death, if only she would allow me that choice. It's not dying I regret but the fact that, childless, I can only pass our bed down in these pages.

PLAYED OUT

Sun erupts over the humpbacked mountains, etching its image in the ice-encrusted windshields of cars parked outside the San Juan Pueblo Video Gaming Palace. Bent and broke, Kokopelli slips out the back door with nothing but his flute, ready to crawl back into the rocks.

THE ONLY DIFFERENCE

—for Tony Burciaga

The only difference between us is the rate at which
we are dying, I think, as I double-clutch past a fish-
erman fixing a flat near the banks of the Río Embudo.
Even that distinction, of course, is as uncertain as
the clouds watercolored in this February sky. Yet the
ice has already begun to surrender to the spring stir-
ring in the junipers, and the only difference is that
you have given up the fear that continues to drive me.

A crescent moon contemplates me with pursed
lips as I finger the missing *medalla* of the Virgin
of Guadalupe I relinquished to the river instead
of my life. "All rivers are born of the sea," wrote the
Mexican poet who, like me, lost both of his fathers.
In answer to your question, I can never know what
these words will say, for even as I set them in ink
they go flooding back to the blackness from which
we were born (or to which we are bound, which,
in the end, is the opposite way of saying the
same thing).

TRIPTYCH

1

Every Sunday morning for a month we received
the same obscene phone call. When my wife
would answer—Sunday mornings the phone is
always for her—a young male voice would address
her by name (or a birdlike approximation thereof):
"Mrs. Seagull, you wanna fuck?" At last, determined
to put a stop to the calls, I picked up the phone
when it rang at the hour most good Catholics are
giving the sign of peace. "Is Mrs. Seagull there?"
the voice asked. "Who *is* this?" I growled into the
mouthpiece. "Gerald Martínez," the voice replied
without hesitation. "Who *is* it?" my wife asked as
I handed her the phone. "Gerald Martínez," I
shrugged. "Mrs. Seagull," Gerald said when my
wife answered—"you wanna fuck?"

2

On my knees in the front pew of the nave, I prayed
the rosary, trying to keep my eyes from returning to
the stark profile in the open casket at the altar. As the
rezador rattled off the Our Father, I leaned over to
the niece at my side and whispered, "Was he Catho-
lic?"—meaning, of course, our late relative. But she,
not hearing the past tense in my verb, assumed I was
asking about her husband seated to her left. "Not
anymore," she replied, not comprehending why I
had to hide my face in my folded hands to keep
from drowning out the Glory Be with laughter.

3

For the first time in its four hundred year history,
the city of Santa Fe is less than fifty percent Hispanic.
New Yorkers and Californians have even taken over
the Catholic cemetery in Tesuque, the village just
north of the capital where the median price for a
house hovers near three-quarters of a million dollars.
Forced out of their native mountains, *nuevomexicanos*
have finally come to understand why their ancestors
named them the *Sangre de Cristos.*

He was shot as he was leaving the lounge,
only twenty-nine years old, they say his wife
went mad with grief, taking her three children
out to the cemetery in the middle of the night to
talk to their father, and now his mother spends
her days weeping with the television on, a cry
primordial as the death that awaited him as it
waits for us all, just outside the door.

In the Best Western lobby, four beer-bloated rough-
necks wolf down complimentary Little Debbies,
stationed around an ashtray already filling up with
Marlboro butts. "Ya cain't even understand em
when they tauk on the phone," complains the
apparent *jefe* of the group—or at least the one whose
tee-shirt is suffering the greatest stress. Lumbering
into a set of trucks emblazoned with the legend
"Santa Fe Drilling" (though the license plates are
from Illinois), the men roll to work over the muddy
and nearly motionless Río Grande. Headed for the
Santa Teresa Port of Entry, they pass by the Sunland
Park Elementary School, built on the site of an old
medical waste dump. An occasional syringe still turns
up on the playground where 98% of the student pop-
ulation is Mexican or Mexican-American. A sixth-
grader whose teacher moonlights as a belly dancer
at the Las Cruces Wal-Mart leads the school in the
morning Pledge of Allegiance and the singing of
"America" over the intercom. "Oh beautiful for
spacious skies," the five hundred *niños* sing, their
thin voices rising like birds through the brown cloud
billowing over the border that the quartet of pot-
bellied drillers are about to cross.

GHOST RANCH SALES RING

The old men in battered straw hats lean against
the fence at the Ghost Ranch Sales Ring. Nearly
immaterial in their cuffed and sagging levis, they
watch the buyer scrutinizing their aging cows, the
last remnants of the herds that once defined them.
Still as the hot dust that hangs over the corral, the
old men wait, not so much to see how little they
will receive for their animals, as to ward off,
for a few hours more, the long ride home in
an empty truck.

AMOR DE LEJOS

Amor de lejos es para los pendejos.
—Traditional New Mexican saying

Love at terrible distances sends the flesh up in
smoke. Such passion builds shrines in the wilderness,
forces simple men to find saints in uprooted trees.
Impeccably foolish, I keep falling in love with the
unattainable for the pure poetry of the plunge.

NIPPED IN THE BUD

A false spring in February duped the daffodils into
an early appearance this year. Now the snow has
halted their growth, the lemon drop buds wrapped
snug in their shoots like children bundled up in
overcoats.

When Joe was an altar boy during this frigid
and blustery season of Lent, his mother would wet
down his unruly hair before he set out walking to
the Santa Cruz Church to serve the seven A.M.
mass. The irascible Catalonian priest would be
well into the Act of Contrition before the ice had
melted from Joe's frozen hair.

I must need the sun more than I fear the paralyzing
penance of the frost. Otherwise, my heart long ago
would have taught me to keep my head underground.

THIS TIME AROUND

Hurtling into the Jicarilla night on a road I share
with insomniac jackrabbits, I search for your eyes in
the blackness like a mystic tortured by the dream in
which he is on the verge of seeing the face of the
translucent figure at the door, but the instant before
she turns, he awakens. Night leads into deeper night,
but this time around I refuse to fall asleep at the
wheel.

DECIDUOUS SCAR

Whose idea was it to climb so high, you ask, but the ache in my lungs has stolen my voice. Though our trails diverged far below, we have ended up at the same shivering aspen tattooed with our initials. The deciduous scar cuts deep, but the heart-shaped hurt has never stopped growing.

Satisfied as Buddha, tía Bernie would sit in velvet
clouds of tobacco smoke, defying her doctors' orders
with a smile in her eyes magnified by the thick lenses
of her spectacles. *"Poco veneno no mata,"* she would
say, helping herself to another sugary *bizcochito* in
her advanced diabetic condition — "A little poison
won't kill you."

Far worse, tía Bernie understood, was the *veneno* of
separation and self-denial, so she held onto her sweets
and her stories, populating her eight by twenty-five
foot trailer with the *novios* of her youth, the divorced
husbands, jealous *comadres,* and beloved boy she
dressed up in a cowboy outfit and raised as though
he were her own *hijo.*

Never alone in her solitude, tía Bernie didn't dis-
appear in her passing, as she left behind a wealth
of *chistes* and sayings that keep conjuring her up.
"Oh, Dios," she says, rolling another cigarette and
filling my ears with her laughter — "a little death
can't stop my story."

STRANGELY STRIPPED

Driven out of bed by dreams, I wait in the dim
light of a fire for the dawn. "How long have you
been naked?" I asked the man in my dream.
"Seven years," he replied, and I shuddered to
feel his craving in my bones.

In their language, the Tewas call the peak outside
my awakening window, the "Mountain Without
Clothes." It is an old hunger that has left me
strangely stripped in the morning chill, never
satisfied in these shadows. Never fully clothed.

PORQUE ME DUELEN LAS MANOS

Porque me duelen las manos de tanto no tocarla,
me duele el aire herido que a veces soy.
—Jaime Sabines, *"La Tovarich"*

The gravest hurt is the one I have never known,
the irrevocable loss that would force me to prize each
wounded breath. Such is the pain of the boulders
unbuffeted by the wind, the rocks languishing for
the kiss of the rain that never falls—the wind and
the rain that, over unimaginable time, could at last
wear an opening in this stony heart.

LAST CHANCE FOR GAS

Following the falling sun, I meander off the map
past a pair of deserted gas pumps. Ahead, a stop sign
is sprawled at an impotent angle, stopping nothing.
Close to empty, I will soon be running on light.

switchback

ORIGIN OF SPECIES

In Gallinas Canyon, patriarchal oaks lift their arms
in supplication to the sky while I sit in the shade of a
promontory stubby as my grandfather's thumb. Vans
broadcasting rap music rumble past, but my eyes
are fixed on a pair of hawks pirouetting against the
sun. Time seizes up when I step into the stream,
convinced I am in the wrong race.

Lizard darts across the washboard road in front of
my heaving car. A good sign, like the clouds roiling
in the sky. Like the music rising again in my throat.

On just such a moon-splashed evening, I set out
walking across town to her apartment, twelve-string
guitar in hand. Sitting cross-legged on the hardwood
floor, I played my full repertoire of love songs to that
lady with the smoky smile. Too hungry for each other
to finish dinner, we were soon bucking together on
the bare floor, scattering plates of food and upending
the guitar in a discordant crash. Afterwards, as we lay
naked next to the peas and porkchops beneath a
window streaming with light, she asked how many
women I had been with. I lied, of course, even
though I knew that she knew it had been my first
time, over so soon yet still lingering thirty years
later under the spell of this virgin moon.

WHITTLING AWAY

Kingston, New Mexico, "Home of the Spit
and Whittle Club," lies on the apron of the Gila
National Forest where native trout shimmer under
the rocks of the Iron River and javelinas lead their
litters across the highway at midnight. "ANCING"
reads the broken window of the El Rancho Bar,
eroding now like the mountains of tailings at the
Santa Rita mine, row after row of copper dinosaur
toes. Lost on North Mineral Street, I realize that,
for a few moments at least, I do not need anything
at all.

Not long after her father's death, Teresa sat,
entranced, on the cottonwood *canoba* as his
spirit circled around her in the form of a
yellow butterfly.

When she was a child, doña Luisa watched
her *abuela* walking out to the corn field and
filling her apron with so many butterflies that
she began to rise into the air.

Dozing under cottony skies beside the Río del
Pueblo, I think of the old Chinese mystic who
awoke on the banks of such a sleepy stream after
dreaming he was a butterfly. The only problem
was, he could not decide if he was the man who
had dreamt he was a butterfly, or if he was a
butterfly now dreaming he was a man.

And what dreamer must be imagining me on such
an unimaginable day, I wonder, as I open my eyes
to start dreaming.

DOUBLE IMAGE

Parked in the shadow of the Laguna Church, I gaze
at a row of sunflowers bowing with the burden of too
much summer in their heads. He grinds up beside
me, the tires of his black Bonneville sputtering gravel
like a hard rain of holy water. In his Megadeath tee-
shirt and kerchief headband, the Pueblo youth stares
five hundred years back at me. His mirrored sun-
glasses reflect the walls of the church behind me—
twin visions of a white-washed world suspended in
a cobalt sky.

SWITCHBACK

As I climb the steep switchbacks on four cylinders at fall, I feel the mountain quaking beneath my tires. Around the bend, a porcupine waddles across the asphalt and disappears into a prehistoric opening in the aspens. My fingers are quivering as I grasp the wheel, hard, as though I could keep death from shaking me free.

A NEW ORCHARD

You were bucking haybales when many of your
contemporaries were sitting in rest homes, and you
could still walk up the side of a mountain *a pesar de
todos los años que llevaba encima* — in spite of the
years you lugged along on your back. But nothing
astonished me more than the fact that you were
planting peach trees in your eighties. Only half your
age, I already balk at the thought of a new orchard as
I go blundering from one crisis to the next. Perhaps
all of mid-life is a crisis, and, with luck, one finally
gets too old to worry about it anymore. Then, like
you, I might be able to plant trees free of any hope
of fruit.

THIS LAND A BRIDE

It is not the land but what is no longer left in the
land that imparts beauty to the Bisti, this wind-
riddled countenance of stone extraordinary as
Vicentita Espinoza's furrowed face as she poses
for a photograph next to her propped-up husband
and jokes about raffling him off for their seventy-
fifth wedding anniversary, this land a bride
rendered radiant by erosion.

LIGHTING UP

Six A.M. at the Wagon Wheel Cafe. Bestubbled
wheat farmers with tobacco-stained teeth and Dekalb
Seed Corn caps welded to their skulls crouch over
meaty hands as if the wind were blowing at their
backs. They eat eggs greasy side up and talk cattle
through a haze of cigarette smoke.

Bonnie, the waitress, stubs out her own Camel and
addresses the cook over the sizzling sausage. Got a
new dye job on her hair, did it herself because she
wasn't about to go to no hairdresser without no
pockets in his pants—says—she don't care if she
does look like a blueberry, when you get as old as
she is, you can have any color of hair you want.

Methodically making the rounds, she refills all the
coffee cups and calls everyone honey while, outside
the east window, the sun strikes a match to the yawn-
ing clouds.

A LITTLE MORE
EVERY MORNING

A band of *calacas* grin back at me from the shelf
where they clang cymbals, hawk newspapers and lasso
snorting bulls with their skeletal hands, rawboned
jaws flapping and bobbing *en una sonrisa de muerte*,
the same smile curling at my lips a little more every
morning in the mirror.

It's the space between thoughts, that sliver
of light outlining the dark door of our dreams.
It's the moment before hello, the instant that
belongs to the eyes. It's the synchronicity of
separate heartbeats—recognition, desire,
poetry.

STARSTRUCK ON A
NEW MEXICAN NIGHT

Another time Coyote came sneaking up on the First
People. They were busy laying out the stars on the
Celestial Blanket—four billion here, four billion
there, all in perfect order. Never content to be an
extra, Coyote just had to steal the scene. Clamping
onto the heavenly tapestry with his teeth, he snarled
a show tune and shook it this way and that until, at
last, the stars were all scattered in the sky. Coyote
has been howling with laughter every night since
and chaos has come to be the order of the day.

CHAIN REACTION

Two bicyclers pause for a kiss on the overlook of
the Valle Grande, their helmets a pair of hungry
electrons colliding as our mouths melt down and
the heart reaches critical mass.

INDEPENDENCE DAY

There is a photograph of my grandfather and me,
taken somewhere in the Colorado Rockies. It is the
Fourth of July, according to the numerals penciled on
the back of the image—his birthday. I am recently
two years old, on my first outing in the mountains,
no doubt, as I was born on the flat lands, in the
wrong place. My grandfather already knows this,
supporting me as we walk away from the camera.
Heading into the pines, we may never return.

CARICIA

Not far from the ruins, I caress the edge of a toppled
boulder as if it were the soft swell of your cheek.
Rain falls on the sandstone face that drinks up the
drops indistinguishable from my tears.

GRACE PERIOD

All I ask is the time to reconsider the things I
cannot change, a few final moments, not to repent,
but to contemplate, like a climber, the flow of my
life unraveling through the canyons below. I fear
nothing more than a sudden and meaningless
ending: a traffic accident, lightning striking from
an unscathed sky, literally dying for love.

INTIMATE
CONSTELLATION

Cricket gone crazy under the climbing roses, chirp-
ing as if the stars were still shining through all this
light illuminating the feathery snow that bursts from
the cottonwoods along the ditch whose waters lap
over the thirsty earth like my tongue tracing the
constellation in your thighs.

STRANDED

He was working on her roof when the ladder fell and
stranded him all afternoon. Bellowing and cursing,
he stomped on the roof, for he knew the old man was
in the house below, unless the bastard had croaked.
At last, he gave up, sat down on the freshly graveled
tar paper and thought about how fitting it was, just
like her to leave him high and dry like this. But,
then, the old man came stumbling out the front
door.

"Didn't you hear me, goddamit?"

"Sure, I heard you, but I thought the world
was coming to an end, so I stayed in bed."

Fifteen minutes later, after the arthritic old man
finally got the ladder in place, he scrambled off
the roof, and all he could think, as he descended
two rungs at a time, was that he would never fall
in love again.

Orphaned from the yellow cliffs, these sandstone
pearls have been sculpted over millennia by the
relentless wind. Like the kiva I gaze into as I write
these lines, like the earth that rolls beneath my feet,
these rocks are round as God.

In Ojo Sarco, six men huddle like surgeons around
an uphooded Chevy pickup, drinking the inevitable
Buds and smoking in the unfiltered light. I wave as
I drive past, having only recently emerged from the
fog in the valley like a soul catapulting out of a
broken-down body. What spark burns inside me
like the sun in this transparent sky?

ONE OF THESE RUTTED
LOGGING ROADS

A quarter of a century ago, we pulled our VW off
one of these rutted logging roads and made love in
the Black Mountains. Though it is business in Silver
City that has set me retracing the route of our elope-
ment, I imagine the back seat once again filled with
the sum total of our worldly possessions—several
boxes of books, a guitar, the black clay pot your
great-grandmother made, the single sleeping bag
we shared under the trio of comets that hung in the
Guaymas sky, and the collection of Beatle albums
we pawned for bread, sodas and just enough Pemex
for the return journey home. Twenty-five years pass
as quickly as I pen them, but I am still trading my
music to get back to you.

LAMENT TO SAN ISIDRO

I lost my appetite listening to the California "cowboy"
at the next table talking about his property in the
mountains above the Abiquiú Inn Restaurant.
Loudly, he mispronounced the names that still
resonate in my heart: la Cañada Bonita, Mesa de
Poleo, Cañón, places I once knew at your side on
horseback, on foot, or rattling over unmapped roads
in the old Dodge—el Pinabetal, los Chihuahuenses,
Coyote, the red mesas and secluded *vegas* your
grandfather first settled that now belong to men
who mangle their names.

San Isidro, I only worked on the Sabbath because
these newcomers keep plowing us over. Here I am,
juggling several jobs, yet the best I can do is an
occasional dinner out that only serves to disillusion
me. Now more than ever, I could use an angel with
a strong back, but, San Isidro, you keep sending us
worse and worse neighbors.

On barebacked horses we raced up the volcanic
spine of the Black Mesa, defying the monster with
his appetite for rebellious children. Is it his taste
for revenge that has caused him to devour all these
years? Even now I am consumed by the ghosts still
galloping in my blood, consumed by my memory
of the smell of the wind in our hair.

ALAS NEGRAS

"José always wanted to fly."
—from the eulogy at the funeral of Fr. José Rodríguez

You wrapped yourself in priestly vestments against
the cold diagnosis, offering the brief balance of your
life on the altar of the one who also died for love.
Clothed in black feathers, you rose to your last role,
but the sun, like an inexorable virus, consumed your
wings. Only in crashing to earth could you finally
fly, disintegrating into naked light at the moment
of reentry.

THE OTHER SIDE

Notebook in hand, I sit at the grassy edge of the Río
Chiquito and listen to a hidden thrush sing away the
sun. The water rushes away with my thoughts until,
finger by finger, I relinquish my pen. Gently, rain
begins to fall on this college-ruled page, blotting out
the earlier drafts of my life. A willow arches over the
stream like my longing for the words beyond words,
nearly touching the other side.

THE END OF
MANY THINGS

—for Tito

"Pueblo life was timeless. I felt like I had lived
forever and I was going to live forever," you say,
leaving the lecture hall to follow your father up the
mountain before the atomic weapons facility fenced
it off, for *Gia* had said you would need four deer to
get through the winter and, like your father, you
would not return home without them, not in those
times when you still raised your own beans and
corn near the ruins of your ancestors' cliff-dwelling
village, long before your father started working up
on that same hill, building frame houses for the
scientists in order to earn the paycheck that would
buy the liquor that left him passed out at your feet
on the banks of the river.

"I saw the end of many things," you say, drawing
yourself back with a deep breath while several
laboratory employees in the audience glance at
their watches.

SURVIVOR

While riding out the storm of God's silence, I ran aground in the desert. What can I do but abandon ship and turn my eyes back to the sky? I set out under this mute ocean of stars, charting a new course on the latitude of floundering hope, the longitude of my shipwrecked soul.

Compared to your sons, I had it easy. They were
barely boys when you sent them into the night to
fetch water from the creek. Hidden in the scrub oaks
outside the cabin, you hooted like an owl, chuckling,
no doubt, to watch them sloshing up the hill with
the heavy pails in their hands and a pack of *brujas*
at their backs.

My initiation took place on a brilliant July morning
as we walked into the forest, searching for calves in
the *cañadas* above your ranch. I was puffing behind
as you trudged up the rocky slopes and over the fallen
pines, doubling my stride even though you tripled
my age. As my thoughts floated off with the cumulus
clouds scarcely an arm's length over our heads, I'd
pause now and then to pick up a sliver of quartz or
smoky flint, careful never to lose sight of you, a work-
shirted figure crunching through the *pinoreales*.
An hour later, my lungs bursting and my pockets
bulging with *piedras*, we finally stopped on a
plateau. As a smile played below your mustache,
you instructed me to go back the way we had come

while you would circle ahead and meet me back at the cabin. You were gone before I could get a word out, though I don't know what I would have said.

Fear pounded in my ears as I took my first tentative steps back, desperately trying to recognize something familiar in the faceless boulders and the unfriendly Ponderosas. Even the birds circling dizzyingly overhead seemed to sense I was lost. Still, I would have preferred meeting up with a black bear to seeing the look on your face if you had been forced to rescue me.

Miraculously, I found my own way down to the fenced pasture of the ranch. Whether it was luck or sheer terror that led me back, I'll never know, but from that day forward, I have always kept track of my surroundings. Wherever I go, from Manhattan to Nageezi, I keep my eyes peeled, my ears opened, my senses tuned. Though I may not understand exactly where I'm going, I do have a strong sense of where I've been. And I always remember how to get home.

Anasazi wall soars over my head, red stones mortised by the wind. A doorway is etched in the clouds, but I can't construct a sentence to reach it. When I am finally done with these words, I will step into the sky.